MMA UNSCRIPTED

BEHIND THE SCENES OF AMERICA'S HOTTEST SPORT

TRIUMPH
BOOKS

MMA UNSCRIPTED

BEHIND THE SCENES OF AMERICA'S HOTTEST SPORT

This book is available in quantity at special discounts for your group or organization. For further information, contact:
Triumph Books

TRIUMPH
BOOKS

542 South Dearborn Street
Suite 750
Chicago, Illinois 60605
(312) 939-3330
Fax (312) 663-3557
www.triumphbooks.com

Printed in U.S.A.
ISBN: 978-1-60078-317-3

Concept by Robert Pittman
Written by Chris Staab
Additional writing by Bobby Pittman, RJ Clifford and Clyde Gentry
Story Editor by Clyde Gentry
Copy Editor by Nicole Pittman
Photo Editor by Chris Staab
Layout and Design by Lisa Williams

Photos courtesy of RJ Clifford, Scott Harrison, Justin Hawkins, Tracy Lee, Rick Lee, Jim Manalisay, Bobby Pittman, Nicole Pittman and Chris Staab

table of
CONTENTS

INTRODUCTION

Welcome to *MMA Unscripted,* your visual adventure through one of the most informative and captivating television shows on the great sport of Mixed Martial Arts!

MMA Worldwide has for years proven to be one of the best resources for all things MMA through their two magazines, *MMA Worldwide* and *TapouT,* website (www.mmaworldwide.com), digital editions, tours, radio and every other facet of media entertainment. When it was time to take our company to a new level and into people's living rooms via their television sets, we knew we were making history. *MMA Worldwide* aired on HDNet, the home for MMA, for ten weeks and was one of their most popular MMA shows.

When the dust settled, the cameras turned off and the editing finished, we had so much more we wanted to show the MMA fans that just would not fit into ten 1/2 hour episodes. When all was said and done, we realized it would be a crime to let the fans not see and experience what we the crew had the opportunity to enjoy. So we took everything off the cutting room floor and glued it into what you are holding right now. The best of *MMA Worldwide.*

You get to see behind the scenes photos of all of your favorite MMA Worldwide moments like training in Las Vegas with Wanderlei Silva and hanging out with Forrest Griffin. Meet some of the best personalities in the sport like Bruce Buffer, Frank Trigg and Tom Atencio. And remember the legendary father of Brazilian jiu-jitsu, Helio Gracie through our special tribute.

We put together the best crew to handle the best MMA adventures we could come up with. With Bobby leading the way, Joker laughing uncontrollably, Freddy telling us what's what and me just trying to get it all done right, each of us, in our own special way, bring the side of Mixed Martial Arts most fans do not get to see right into your hands. We love this sport and all that is has done. Like anything held dear, it needs to be remembered. If you are a fan of our show, like reading our magazines or just want a fresh look on MMA, I think you should turn the page and see what's in store.

Trust me when I say this is only the beginning of what **MMA Worldwide** has in store for the ever growing MMA fandom. I hope you enjoy reading this as much as we enjoyed making it.

RJ Clifford
Editor, Fighter, Crew Member, Fan

CHAPTER 1

HISTORY

Just like many in the MMA world, the Pittman family sat in amazement on November 12, 1993, as they witnessed Royce Gracie take on all comers in the very first UFC. From that moment on, Robert Sr.'s love for martial arts was rejuvenated and he soon began training at the Gracie Academy in Torrance, California with Royce and Rorion Gracie.

With his son Bobby following in his footsteps, the two began the ritual of training together whenever possible. Bobby eventually competed in wrestling, jiu-jitsu and boxing, and even though his competition days came to an end, his love for MMA remained strong. Combining their passion for the sport and Robert Sr.'s decades of experience in the printing industry, the two decided to start a magazine devoted to martial arts.

At the time of their first discussions to launch the magazine, mixed martial arts was still in what many called "The Dark Ages" and many wondered if it was nothing more than a fad. Mainstream sponsors seemed nowhere in sight; MMA was still criticized throughout the country. With this in mind, Robert was hesitant to launch a full-blown MMA magazine and instead chose to go with a name he thought would have more mass appeal. He chose to go with *Bodyguard* with the slogan, "Protect your home, protect yourself, protect your family." His vision was to use the new techniques being developed in MMA to show the average person how to stay safe in the real world. Things were on track until he put Bobby in charge.

Robert and Sheree Pittman

With Robert giving Bobby the authority to choose who and what went into the magazine, it wasn't long before the pages of *Bodyguard* were filled with faces like Bas Rutten, Randy Couture and other famous fighters. Of course, the Editor-in-Chief had to keep his dad happy with the occasional story on Navy SEALS, bodyguards and other experts who would share their stories and knowledge about personal safety, but it was clear that Bobby had other plans. "I always saw MMA being a huge sport and wanted to go that direction from day one, but I had to ease my dad into it for a while. Him and I throwing arm bars on each other in the garage is one thing, but asking him to invest his money in something that was still seen in such a negative light by so many in corporate America was definitely not going to be easy," explains Bobby.

As time passed, MMA continued to grow and so did the Pittman's relationships within the MMA world. The content of the magazine kept evolving and Robert soon realized which direction the company was headed. Looking back, Robert says, "Starting out, we didn't really know what to put in the magazine. We had a ton of ideas, but we basically just had to try things out and see what our readers responded to. It didn't take long for me to see the want and the need for the first magazine devoted to MMA." With father and son now seeing eye to eye on the direction, it was time to change the name.

After a column was published for a name-change contest, Bobby received a call from one of the owners of Tapout, Dan Caldwell, also known as Punkass. With Tapout already an advertiser in the magazine, Dan and Bobby had been in contact for quite some time and both shared similar ideas on the sport. After a few meetings, the deal was done and the Pittman's re-launched with *Tapout*.

Tapout Magazine was an instant hit with readers and advertisers alike and the magazine grew leaps and bounds. It wasn't long before Bobby, being the dreamer that he is, had ideas for expansion. The first order of business was assembling a crew consisting of Bobby, RJ Clifford (who had taken on the role of Editor-in-Chief), Freddy George (who helped launch the magazine) and MMA fighter Michael "The Joker" Guymon. Bobby's plan was to hit the road via tour bus and go on a guerilla marketing campaign to take the magazine to the next level. Only one problem stood in his way. The agreement between the Pittman's company and Tapout restricted certain uses of the name. Tapout's owners also felt this may be a conflict with their future TV show where they would also hit the road in a tour bus. The solution: *MMA Worldwide*.

"When I dreamt of going on tour, I grew dead set on the idea. After all, the entire crew we had and everyone else I knew working in this industry had literally come straight out of the gyms and into the MMA business. It's like everyone who got on the mats in the early days got bit with the MMA bug and we all went on a mission to build a sport out of our passions. If we were going to the next level, we had to connect with the next generation of MMA fans and show them just what our team and company was all about, the same way the Gracie's showed me what their family and jiu-jitsu was about. I couldn't let the situation with the Tapout name stop me, so we had to launch a brand of our own. I'll always be proud to publish *Tapout Magazine*, but launching *MMA Worldwide* opened up a world of possibilities," Bobby recalls.

The Pittman Family at MMA Worldwide Booth.

With the new magazine, a tour bus and the crew assembled, the MMA Worldwide Road Show began. Staying on the road for over four months, the crew traveled up and down the West Coast hitting every gym and event they could get to, gathering content for the magazines and building valuable relationships along the way. Bobby stated, "The tour was one of the best things we could have done. The amount of contacts and relationships we gained could keep our business going forever, but there was something far more important that happened. Living with those jackasses on a tour bus for that long showed me exactly where we needed to go. Anyone who came in contact with the crew saw that if you had cameras rolling, you had gold."

Immediately following the conclusion of the tour, the Pittman's launched their TV venture by producing the first season of *MMA Worldwide* for a local Southern California channel, KDOC. With that first season receiving the station's highest ratings ever for a new show, the MMA Worldwide Crew seemed to have found their calling. Robert Sr. hit the phones to sell the show to a larger network and it wasn't long until HDNet was onboard and Season Two was underway. Bobby says, "Having the show on HDNet is really a testament to how far we have come. I still watch HDNet as a fan and now to see our show play right before *Inside MMA* with Bas Rutten is truly an honor. The future is definitely bright for *MMA Worldwide* and *Tapout Magazine*."

Legendayr Judo master Gene LeBell working our booth.

Greg Jackson and Keith Jardine at our MMA Worldwide booth.

CHAPTER **2**

THE CREW

For over six years MMA Worldwide has grown WITH this sport. *MMA Worldwide* and *Tapout Magazine* have brought you industry coverage like none other. NO ONE else brings fans closer to the action and to fighters people pay good money to see.

Now with a show airing on HDNET, MMA Worldwide has a new vehicle to help bring this sport to life. Fans get an inside look at what it takes to put together a magazine and bring back the stories that make MMA a worldwide phenomenon.

In Season One of *MMA Worldwide*, we followed five MMA personalities, each unique in his connection to the sport.

RJ Clifford, the magazine's editor, decides who gets interviewed, which gyms get covered and which events the fans want to see. On top of all this, RJ is also an up and coming fighter whose knowledge of the sport makes him the commentator EVERY promoter wants!

Robert and Bobby Pittman is the father/son team in charge of the MMA Worldwide empire. Robert, a Kung Fu San Soo blackbelt, has been a passionate fan of MMA since day one. When his son Bobby, a former wrestler and student of Royce (pronounced Hoyce) Gracie suggested they start a magazine, Robert stepped up to the plate.

Fast forward six years.

Bobby Pittman, Rick Lee, Mike "Joker" Guymon, RJ Clifford and Freddy George after RJ's fight.

Now Bobby hosts the most informative mixed martial arts TV show on any network, bringing you stories of the fighters outside the cage and exposed for our cameras.

Through the years making both magazines, this trio has made many friendships with some of the sport's most colorful characters.

Enter **Mike Guymon**, but forgive him if he doesn't answer to that name; his friends know him as "Joker". He may be smiles on-camera, but when it comes to MMA, he does NOT take the sport lightly. One seldom sees the process it takes to become a fighter, and even more rare, a champion. As the King of the Cage 170-pound champion, Joker knows that process well. Follow Joker as he teams up with the crew balancing time as an MMA fan covering the sport with time as a cage warrior, king of his domain.

Last but not least is **Freddy George**.

EVERYBODY knows Freddy. He is co-owner of the CSW Training Center in Fullerton, CA. Something you'll learn about Freddy very quickly is that he knows everything. He knows striking. He KNOWS jiu-jitsu, and most importantly, he knows how to fix the RV.

The RV is arguably the sixth cast member. Travel state to state in this beast and you will see that she has a personality of her own. Still she gets the MMA Worldwide crew from Point A to Point B on time....well, usually. Some things are just beyond her control.

Bobby Pittman at Zion National Park.

Freddy
"The Detroit Diesel"
George

HARDCORE

MMA

17

Mike "Joker" Guymon
preparing to defend his belt
at King of the Cage.

RJ Clifford at his 2nd passion, commentating an MMA fight. Next will be his 1st passion, MMA Worldwide radio host.

CHAPTER

3

SEASON #1

With Bobby Pittman Jr. always dreaming of new ways to expand the business and grow the sport of MMA, a TV show was the next step. After pushing his father Robert for months to dive into the new venture, which is a typical occurrence between the father and son, the two hatched a plan to give the TV world a shot.

After a sales campaign from Robert, the sponsors were onboard and the money was raised to buy a time slot on KDOC, an Orange County independent station. With one sponsorship carrying the obligation of filming an event in the Philippines, the MMA Worldwide crew packed their bags and Season One was underway. Hopes were high for the trip as the crew was sure they were bound for a week of adventure.

From the first moments in the airport, cameras were rolling as fighters and coaches from around the world waited to board their planes. As usual, it was only a matter of time before the crew grew restless and started rolling right in the terminals. For those of you who haven't come across the MMA Worldwide Crew before, this basically means that Freddy George had found a poor, helpless soul to twist into a pretzel while he demonstrated his moves. Legends like Royce Gracie, Gokor Chivichyan and Ricco Rodriguez looked on to get their first taste of the crew. Finally everyone boarded the 20-hour flight and it was off to a foreign land.

MMA WORLDWIDE INC.

AN INSIDE LOOK AT THE FIGHT WORLD

EEKLY TV SHOW • MAGAZINES • WEBSITES • PRODUCT LINE • TOUR GROUP

Working an expo is Bobby's turf.

When asked about the trip, Bobby explains, "Our trip to the Philippines was a truly unforgettable experience. I remember standing in the arena just before the fights started and I couldn't stop thinking of how far MMA had come and how incredible it is to be a part of that growth. We were standing in the same arena that played host to the "Thrilla in Manila" fight with Muhammad Ali and now there's a packed house dying to see MMA. The best part of this job is seeing the sport spread throughout the world and getting to meet these fans who get so much joy from what we have all helped build." After a week of filming, training and wild parties with the many friends they made on their trip, it was time for the crew to head home.

With enough content for three episodes in the can after their trip, the guys got right back to filming. Since Robert and Bobby started their training together with the Gracie family, they were very familiar with the incredible stories they had to share, so it was off to the Gracie Academy where Rener (Rorion's son) played host to the crew.

With RJ Clifford getting ready for his first professional fight, cameras rolled as Rener used his wealth of knowledge to prepare RJ for battle. While Freddy, Mike and RJ shared techniques with Rener, Bobby had other things going on. Growing dizzy and feeling very ill, Bobby abandoned the filming session to head for the crew's tour bus parked outside. It was then that tragedy struck.

Greg Jackson with Sam Strayer of IBN Sports.

Within 24 hours of those first feelings of what felt like a bad flu, the Pittman family and the crew sat in a hospital waiting room as Bobby lay paralyzed from the chest down. Doctors diagnosed the sudden illness as transverse myelitis, a disorder very similar to multiple sclerosis and just as life threatening. Many restless nights were spent as everyone waited, hoping for medications to work and test results to return that would give some hope. After two weeks spent in intensive care, Bobby began the road to recovery and eventually regained mobility. However his battle with the illness continues to this day.

It's needless to say that plans for Season One of *MMA Worldwide* were thrown out the door with the sudden tragedy, but that didn't stop the guys from completing what they had set out to do. While doctors told Bobby he could expect to be living at the hospital for a minimum of three months, the spirit and strength of the entire family came together for what many considered a true miracle. After spending just five days in rehab, Bobby checked out and got back to work, transforming his apartment into a recording studio to create some music for the show.

After some much needed rest and recovery, Bobby rejoined the crew at the HB Ultimate Training Center to film with MMA vet "Razor" Rob McCullough. A few more sessions of filming later and Season One was a wrap. "To be honest, that whole first season of filming was kind of a blur to me. I went through so much going to the hospital and all I could think about was just learning how to walk again. When I look back on it and watch the shows we put together, we had some incredible experiences. Maybe it didn't go exactly as planned, but you know what? We learned how to make a damn show! Bring on Season Two!"

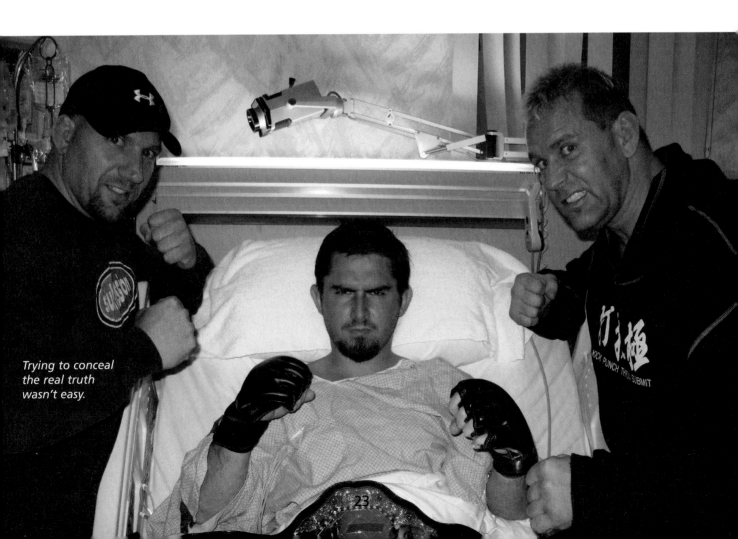

Trying to conceal the real truth wasn't easy.

23

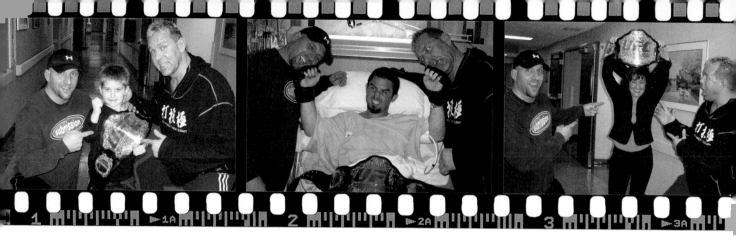

Freddy George made sure to thank everyone for helping Bobby get through this. Freddy is part of the Pittman family!

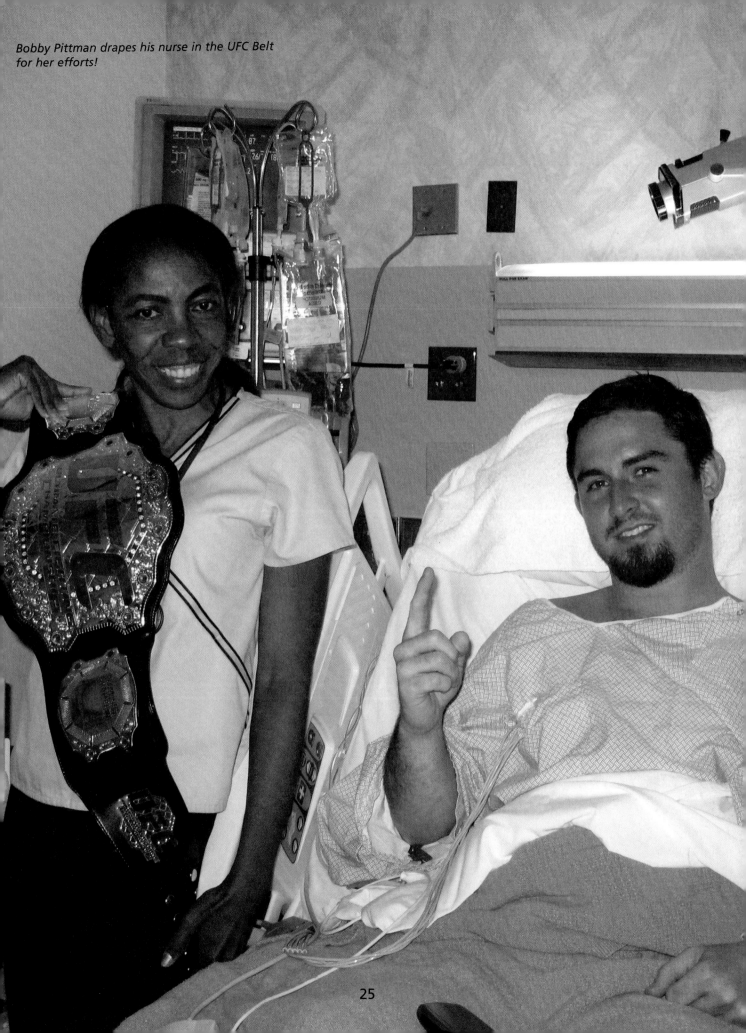

Bobby Pittman drapes his nurse in the UFC Belt
for her efforts!

25

CHAPTER 4

LAS VEGAS

Las Vegas, Nevada is ground zero for any fighter or fight fan looking to get closer to the sport. With so many MMA events, gyms and top team fighters, it only made sense to kick off the season premiere of HDNET's *MMA Worldwide* in Sin City.

UFC 99 seems like the perfect weekend for shooting some incredible footage for the show, especially with Rashad Evans vs. Lyoto Machida headlining at the MGM Grand.

And somewhere in the desert between Los Angeles and Vegas, things started to come together with a phone call from the "Voice of the Octagon" Bruce Buffer. He secures our crew a few spots at the THQ launch party of *UFC: Undisputed*.

At Tabu, a popular nightclub on the strip, people head through the doors to play the game and mingle with some of the famous UFC fighters and personalities featured in the game. In attendance: Bruce Buffer, Jon Fitch, Mike Swick, Hermes Franca and most notably, former UFC light heavyweight champion, Forrest Griffin.

Forrest provides one of the season's most memorable moments when he accepts Bobby's challenge to fight him in the game. Forrest, in an effort to ensure victory, quickly muscles Bobby's controller and proceeds to beat Bobby's defenseless character.

After the party, we call it a night, but not before Wanderlei Silva invited our cameras into his new facility just off the Las Vegas strip.

Upon arriving at Silva's gym, it becomes quickly apparent that the Brazilian was in no mood to play around for the cameras. After all, he was training for an upcoming fight with Rich Franklin. He allows us access for gathering footage, but he has no time to chat. The Axe Murderer was all business on this day.

Originally, Bobby hoped to have a light sparring session with Wandy. He wanted to feel what it was like to be locked in with an animal pacing his cage. But after a brief conversation with Chute Boxe Academy's striking coach Rafael Cordeiro, Bobby realizes our insurance policy would not be enough to cover the damage that was sure to follow.

"Wanderlei is getting ready for his fight. He only has one mode… KILL," says Cardeiro. A typically persistent Bobby Pittman thought maybe Rafael was giving some pretty sound advice. He still wants to have his time in the cage with Wandy, but decides he'll wait until the Brazilian is pushing 60.

Once the crew wraps up at Wanderlei's, it was just about fight time. We headed five quick minutes up the street to the new Tapout Research and Development Training Center. They had purchased the PPV of the fight and were playing it on the big screen at the gym. With names such as Kevin Randleman and Tony Fryklund in the room, we decide it would be advantageous

Wanderlei Silva greets the MMA Worldwide cameras into his new facility in Las Vegas.

Just another day in the
Las Vegas heat

*Refreshing Vegas
eye candy*

to shoot a segment breaking down the key moves in the matches. Tony, a former UFC fighter, gives our cameras and fans an account of how each fight was won.

The fights were amazing and the after parties were in full swing. Actually there may have been a little too much swing. Next morning, Bobby, the show's host, was impossible to wake for our 11:00A.M. interview at Frank Trigg's house. By the time Bobby woke up, we were over an hour late and Frank, true to form, was not letting us off the hook for keeping him waiting. He did the interview, but Frank roasted each crew member from the comfort of his couch.

Tony Fryklund fight analyst extraordinaire breaks moves down like no one can.

*Forrest Griffin cheats by stealing
game controller from Bobby
Pittman and claims victory.*

Once we had enough footage at Trigg's, it was time to "relax" and head over to the Gamma-O pool party in Green Valley. There we caught up with tons of UFC's most feared newcomers, Junie Browning and Matt Brown. They explain that Vegas may have a lot to offer the darker side of their characters, but in the end, they have a job to do. Both admit to getting caught up in the girls, drinks and late Vegas nights earlier in their careers, but now it's time to be serious and make that money.

All in all, Vegas gave us every story we had hoped for the show, and since Vegas never disappoints, she gave us a few stories that we COULDN'T include. But we will always have the memories that made our show's premiere one of the best all season.

Due to explicit material we cannot show you Frank's reaction to our tardy arrival. To see the video out take visit www.mmaworldwide.com.

To keep burglars out of our RV we put a photo of Freddy blasting Joker.

CHAPTER 5

PERSONALITIES

In this episode, we were lucky enough to spend a day with a couple of familiar faces in MMA.

When you think of the UFC, one voice stands out above the crowd. It's probably the most recognized voice in all of MMA and it belongs to the one and only Bruce Buffer.

On any given day, Buffer can be found at the gym, in the sky, or just enjoying a poker game at his house with some friends. In this case, we catch up to Buffer doing all three.

Our second personality is kind of a jack-of-all-trades in the mixed martial arts industry. Tom Atencio helps fighters pay their bills, puts shirts on their backs and gives them a place to fight. He also has no fear stepping into the cage a time or two himself.

Upon entering the Affliction offices, you understand very quickly that this is not your run-of-the-mill day job. In stark contrast from the facade's white exterior, inside you will find the darker and more twisted side of Affliction; Tom Atencio lives in the heart of it all.

We briefly sat for an interview with Atencio about his second MMA fight in Tennessee. We were quickly whisked away down a couple of dark hallways decorated with skulls, angels and guitars in glass cases.

Bruce Buffer jokes
with legendary film
actor James Caan.

At the end of that hallway stood a gigantic sparring ring, but this was no ordinary ring. Not only was its size impressive, but the history behind it made the ring seem larger than life. This was the same ring where Fedor Emelianenko destroyed former UFC champions Tim Sylvia and Andre Arlovski. History has been made inside these ropes and this episode.

At the tail end of Episode 2, Bobby and RJ train with Atencio and Chute Boxe Academy striking coach, Rafael Cordeiro. "Man, Atencio kicked my butt!" said Bobby.

Tom Atencio getting ready to kick Bobby Pittman's butt.

Tom Atencio and Bobby Pittman fight over ad prices.

RJ Clifford and Bobby Pittman
raid the Affliction warehouse.

Bruce Buffer has been the longest standing employee of the UFC. He is also a famous collector of World War 2 weaponry.

FREEMOTION

DUAL
CABLE CROSS

Bruce Buffer trains his core strength to perfect the Bruce Buffer 180.

*Bruce Buffer handing out tickets to
the gun show.*

Ryron Gracie, Riane Gracie, Rose Gracie (children of Rorion Gracie) and Javier Vasquez chat with the crew.

CHAPTER

GRACIES

In the world of Mixed Martial Arts, the Gracie family name is perhaps the most respected. Helio Gracie introduced his style of Jiu Jitsu to the world through his son Royce Gracie, who entered the UFC Octagon and began dismantling opponents two and three times his size. From that day forward, the game had changed. No longer was MMA about two men trading blows on their feet. Now, in order to succeed, you had to be ready for anything… especially fighting on the ground.

Today, Brazilian Jiu Jitsu is studied and respected worldwide. Thanks to the teaching of Helio Gracie, the sport has evolved into a sort of chess game on the canvas. Now, a smaller opponent that is trained in BJJ is just as dangerous as a larger, stronger athlete that relies simply on striking ability.

On January 29, 2009 Helio passed away, leaving behind his sons, who continue keeping his memory alive through his teachings. Though Helio is gone, his spirit lives on anytime two fighters take the competition to the ground.

In the 4th episode of this season, MMA Worldwide paid tribute to Helio, and to the entire Gracie family. The Gracie's have left their fingerprint etched into the history of Mixed Martial Arts, and Helio has been immortalized though his teachings.

Jean Jacques Machado saying goodbye to his late uncle Helio Gracie.

Ryron and Ralek Gracie, the 3rd generation leaders of the Gracie Academy, greet RJ Clifford.

A trip down memory lane through the Gracie Museum at the Torrance Academy.

RJ Clifford and Bobby Pittman
discussing the Gracie Tribute.

CHAPTER 7

TRAINING DAY

Some of the funniest moments this season center around Freddy George. Since he claims to know everything about everything, we thought it would be funny to enter him into "Big" John McCarthy's school for referees, putting his knowledge to the test.

Within minutes of Freddy reffing his first fight, he was already dying to stop the fight, teaching a few moves from his "twister" series. Even McCarthy could do nothing but laugh as George forgot the whole point of the visit in the first place. One thing we do know at MMA Worldwide is that Freddy is no joke when it comes to knowing technique—he is the real deal!

Another amazing thing about Freddy George is the fact he knows EVERYONE! We were able to sit down with Jerry Cain, a long time friend and executive producer of the MMA film, No Rules. Not only did he take the time to speak to us about the project, he also brought out a couple of his expensive toys to play with. Freddy hopped into Jerry's Lambo and headed to the hanger where he keeps his airplane. Bobby and Freddy took to the skies to ride out this segment.

Finishing Episode 4, we offered viewers a glimpse into the future of MMA with the Ruffo brothers, Giovanni (age 7) and Carlos (age 9). Don't call them kids; they are just as scary training with grown men. Between Las Vegas and Southern California, these prodigies have trained with the likes of Randy Couture, Erik Paulson and of course… Freddy George.

How would you like this up your bumper?

Everybody has a big hug for Freddy, even Big John McCarthy.

Freddy George tackles a new job inside the cage- referee.

MMA worldwide

As co-owner of
CSW Training Center,
Freddy George feels at home
inside the cage.

Bobby Pittman psyches himself
up for the fight of his life
against 7 year-old
Giovanni Ruffo.

CHAPTER

SO CAL

This episode was our first opportunity to bring an actual event to the viewers. We had visited the top gyms and had spoken with the legends of the sport, but until Episode 5, we had yet to experience the excitement of a live event. Call to Arms allowed us to share this rite of passage for any MMA fan.

First, we catch up Vladimir Matyushenko, one of the sport's hardest-working men, who allowed us to look into his daily life. For a man who has been it all, including "janitor" which became his moniker, Matyushenko's daily life consists of all kinds of training. After fighting for the UFC, IFC and IFL, he was in the midst of training for another sturdy vet in Jason Lambert at Call to Arms' inauguaral show in Ontario, California.

Joker corners Lambert, Freddy corners Puder, RJ commentates and Bobby goes behind-the-scenes like no one else.

Some of the stories inside the locker rooms were just as compelling as the ones inside the cage as our camera crew was granted All Access. One by one, the fighters return embattled to the locker rooms, some celebrating loud with victory. Winning or losing, fighters deal with the experience differently. As one fighter returned, another would leave for the cage. When it came time for former WWE Tuff-Enuff winner turned MMA pro Daniel Puder to enter the cage, no one could've predicted what happened next.

Vladimir Matyushenko and his son tackle a military training sand hill (open to the public) in Southern California.

As soon as the first bell rang, Puder knew he was in for a fight. Kickboxer Jeff Ford came at him hard with a series of fast punch combinations. But when he tried to kick Puder in the head, he came crashing to the canvas with a fight-ending thud. Puder began to taunt Ford, who suffered a shoulder injury, rousing angry jeers from the crowd.

As Puder took the microphone for his post fight interview, he was booed from the cage. It was a moment that made for great TV, but a nightmare for this newcomer who now sports an 8-0 record. Vladimir Matyushenko won by unanimous decision.

Vladimir Matyushenko prepares to fight Jason Lambert.

Vladimir Matyushenko cools down with a refreshing ice bath after a long day of practice. This is his standard ritual.

Mike "Joker" Guymon joking with his fans outside the Citizens Bank Arena.

58

You want me to say WHAT on air?

Bobby Pittman at center stage.

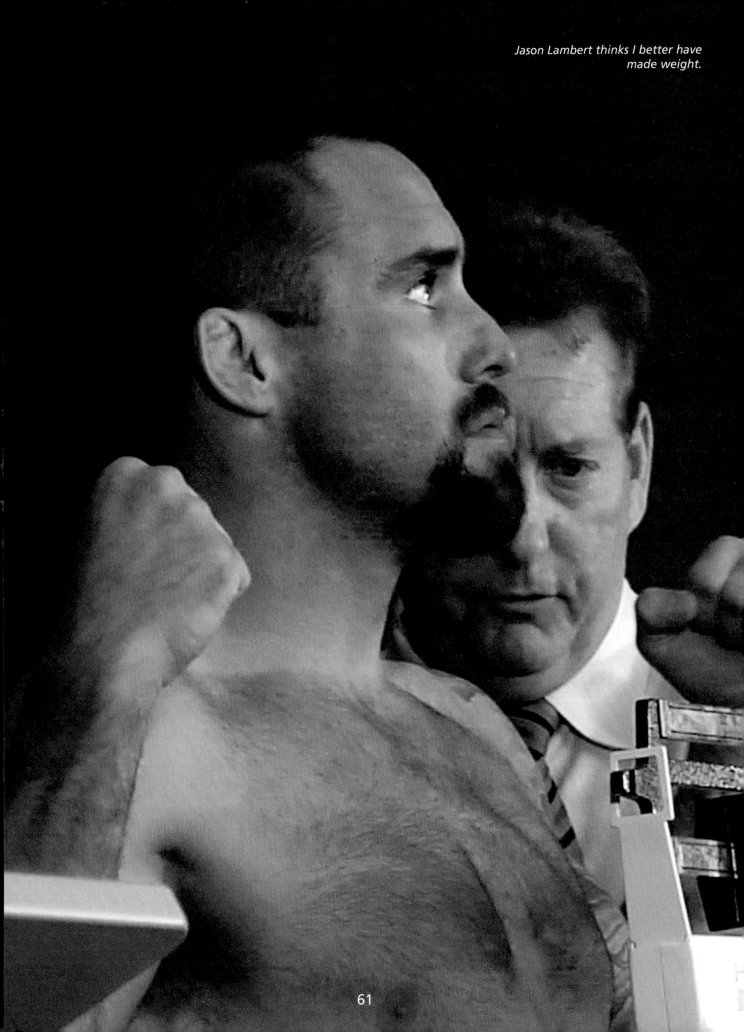

Jason Lambert thinks I better have made weight.

CHAPTER 9

NO CAL

Southern California may have been considered the Mecca of MMA, but in recent years, the Northern part of the state has taken off like wildfire. Frank Shamrock, Cung Le, the Diaz brothers, Gilbert Melendez, Josh Thomson, Jon Fitch, Mike Swick and Josh Koscheck are just some of the names who call the region home, and their combined pedigrees have seen gold many times. Two very distinct schools gave way to this explosion.

When Frank Shamrock left the Lion's Den to carve out his own niche in the late 1990's, he met kickboxing trainer Javier Mendez. Mendez owned the American Kickboxing Academy (AKA) in San Jose and greatly improved Shamrock's striking. But it wasn't until Bob Cook, through his sheer, crazy dedication, came along that the academy really blossomed. Living over three hours away in Norfolk, California, Cook would drive to and from the gym nearly every day while working in the logging industry.

After putting in his time training with Shamrock and Mendez, and going 5-0 as a pro fighter, "Crazy" Bob Cook became a trainer. Today he, along with Brazilian jiu-jitsu ace Dave Camarillo, are two of the top trainers in the sport. Not to be outdone, another team was created in 1999 under the tutelage of Cesar Gracie that would become a fixture in the region. It started with fighters Jake Shields and Gil Castillo, but unlike other BJJ-centric schools, fighters at Cesar Gracie Jiu-jitsu Academy in Pleasant Hills knew how to punch. His team had no problem mixing it up with rival schools in regional shows. Over the years, his team grew to include Nick and Nate Diaz, Gilbert Melendez and David Terrell, but that only makes up their top fighters.

AKA and Cesar Gracie aren't the only two names in town. Cesar Gracie affiliate American Martial Arts Center (Citrus Heights), Nor-Cal Fighting Alliance (Santa Rosa), Fight & Fitness (San Francisco) and Cung Le's Universal Strength Headquarters (Milpitas) are just a few of the schools that are currently training top-notch talent.

Back in the "Dark Ages" of the sport before 2005, the talent was there, but those fight opportunities outside the UFC were barely treading water. Dana White and Zuffa hadn't figured it out yet, regional shows like Gladiator Challenge and International Fighting Championships kept the scene moving, and World Extreme Cagefighting was still an indie show. All eyes were off California as would-be promoters had tried desperately to get the sport legalized in the state, but to no avail. Las Vegas, thanks to the Fertittas, was the only thing on the UFC's mind at the time. California MMA was unfortunately relegated to Indian casinos and unsanctioned by the state.

Kickboxing promoter Scott Coker would change all that on May 10, 2006, when Strikeforce made its debut. Coker was the former K-1 USA figurehead who had developed a relationship with the deep pockets of the San Jose Sharks owners. With his background producing K-1 events in Las Vegas, the California State Athletic Commission gave him and Strikeforce a shot at producing the first legally-sanctioned MMA event in the state.

Nick Diaz tougher in an interview than he is on his opponents.

Held at the HP Pavilion, the event brought together two of the sport's biggest regional stars to collide: Frank Shamrock vs. Cesar Gracie. Shamrock had a falling out with AKA and had started up his own school. Gracie was "rumored" to have had an MMA background but hardly any legit documentation to prove it. His school, instructional DVDs and know-how weren't in question. However, it took just 21 seconds for Shamrock to knock out Gracie in the headliner, which set up rivalries not only between Shamrock and Gracie's camp, but AKA. One record that has yet to be beaten is that of the promotion itself which set an all-time MMA paid attendance record of 17,465.

Strikeforce is one of the top promotions in the world, especially thanks to Pro Elite, whose financial quagmire gave Coker new fighters and distribution through Showtime and CBS. The promotion has also given female fighters a premiere stage, and nearly three years after its inaugural event, Nick Diaz avenged Cesar Gracie by taking out Frank Shamrock a minute shy of five minutes in the second round. Northern California and even Central California are starting to catch up to its Southern counterpart; fans couldn't be happier.

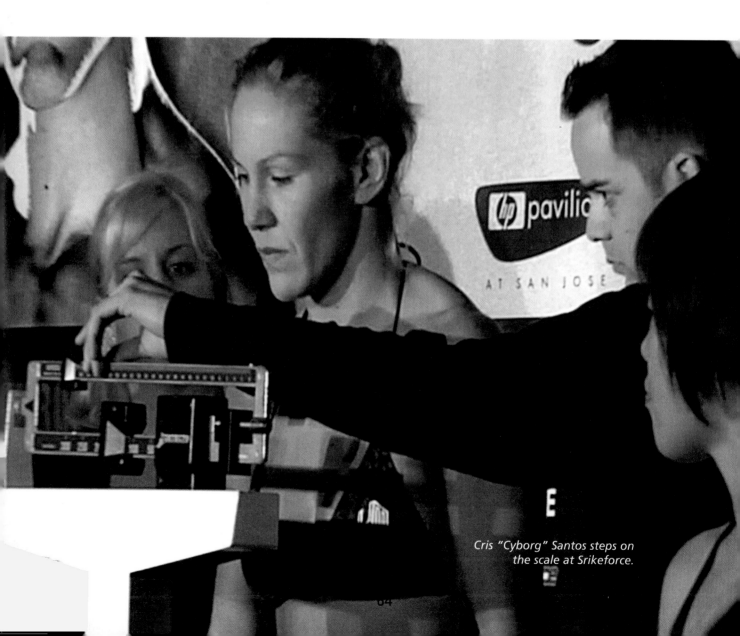

Cris "Cyborg" Santos steps on the scale at Srikeforce.

Herb Dean and the MMA Worldwide crew go way back.

Freddy George serenades RJ Clifford to sleep.

Cung Le talks to the crew about what it takes to be a fight choreographer for film.

RJ Clifford appears on the Sirius Fight Club
radio show hosted by Randy Gordon.

*Cung Le shows Mike "Joker"
Guymon why his scissor takedown is
so lethal.*

CHAPTER 10
MASK

On March 11, 2009, mixed martial arts lost one of its greats.

Charles "Mask" Lewis was a man who knew no definition of boundaries, limitations and the word "can't." Not only did he believe, he could make YOU believe. He was the co-founder of TapouT, a clothing line that has taken the apparel world by storm.

He showed us all that no dream is too big and no idea is too crazy. He was an underdog from the start and built an empire out of the sport of MMA. Along with Dan "Punkass" Caldwell and Scrape, the trio created an entire industry by selling t-shirts out of the back of trunks. But that blossomed into an ongoing presence at MMA shows large and small, and a TV show by the same name on the Versus channel.

In this episode, we take a look back at the life of a champion who never stepped into the ring. Through the people who loved Mask, his essence was remembered in a tribute and short film by Bobby Razak, director at TapouT Films.

Charles "Mask" Lewis looks down at Los Angeles from on top of the Montecito building.

Chuck Liddell showing respect to Mask.

I love you and I'm sorry

Mike "Joker" Guymon breaks down at the crash site.

Charles "Mask" Lewis leaps from the Montecito building while filming his last commercial.

Charles "Mask" Lewis saw no limitations to where Tapout could go.

Image taken from the last commercial Charles "Mask" Lewis ever appeared in, prior to his death.

Skyscrape gets emotional.

Charles "Mask" Lewis
never got to enjoy his
exotic, king-size chairs
and angelic office.

CHAPTER 11

BELLATOR

In the spirit of a live MMA event, the crew set out once again for an incredible night of live fights at Bellator Fighting Championship. Jason Chambers, host of The Human Weapon, gives MMA Worldwide an exclusive backstage look at what it takes to produce a high-end MMA television product.

Bobby had no idea his journey would not end there. He was taken from the production truck to the make-up room to the locker room and then cage side.

The crowd eagerly awaited their hopeful victor of the night...Joe Soto. While waiting for the main event, Bobby ran into the ever-popular and charismatic Thomas "Wild Man" Denny.

At the end of the night, the crowd let go a thunderous roar as their favorite, Joe Soto, strapped the belt across his waist. It was a long and grueling battle, in the end there could only be one winner. Bellator has brought back the ever-loving tournament style where there is only one man standing.

Bellator's famous logo.

Bobby Pittman jokes with Thomas "Wild Man" Denny backstage at the Bellator event.

Bellator fighter walk
the catwal
prepara
for his fi

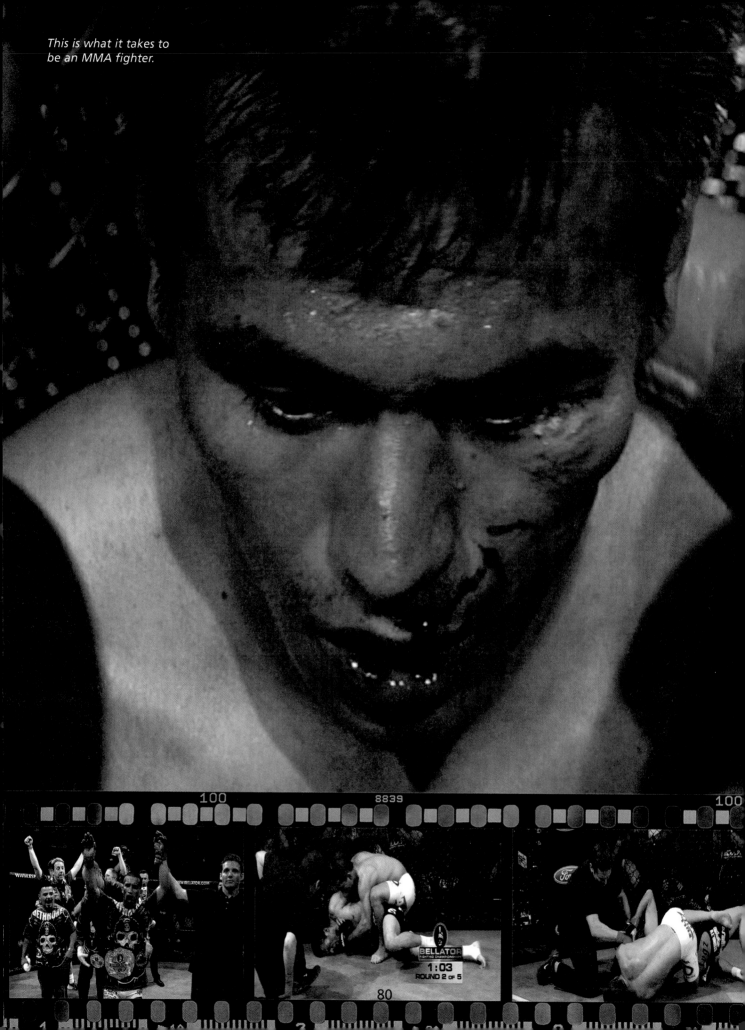

This is what it takes to be an MMA fighter.

*From Human Weapon to Bellator,
Jason Chambers does it all.*

CHAPTER 12

SEASON WRAP UP

After 10 episodes of Las Vegas- style debauchery, bruised faces and long nights in the edit bay, we ended the season with style. Staying true to the magazine, we decided to hold an open audition for Ms. MMA Worldwide and Ms. Tapout.

We started episode 9 at the offices of Tapout clothing where the Tapout photographer directed and photographed six beautiful, aspiring models. In between wardrobe changes, Bobby had a chance to chat with each of the girls about what attracts them to the men of MMA. We were surprised to hear some of their responses! (Visit www.mmaworld-wide.com to hear their comments.)

Cris "Cyborg" Santos was also in the building that day and she talked with us about her victory over the crowd's favorite sweetheart, Gina Carano. Cyborg seemed larger than life when standing next to her, but her demeanor is in direct contrast. She was shy in front of our cameras, and would occasionally burst into nervous laughter. Her and her husband, Mr. Cyborg, eventually relaxed with all the surrounding attention and allowed our photographer an intimate look into their personal lives. They both posed shirtless, embracing each other. It was a rare moment forever immortalized in some unforgettable images.

We also visited the famous Southern California fight club Team Quest when Dan Henderson was getting ready for his fight against Michael "The Count" Bisping. After training, Dan invited our entire crew over to his Temecula Ranch for a BBQ and a couple friendly games of homerun derby in his new batting cage. As usual, Hendo won.

Finally, we met up with fellow crewmember "Joker" as he trained to defend his belt in King of the Cage. It felt as if we were swimming with sharks that day as the Joker's Wild Academy conducted business with vigor. Our cameras caught Joker as he broke down in tears while training. You could hear a pin drop in the room that day, as the pressure of defending his title became obvious to us all. Joker went on to win that fight and is now our first cast member to become a UFC fighter.

With all of the ups and downs, both on and off camera, this was definitely a season to remember. At the end of the day it was a lot of hard work, and such a fitting testament mirroring the trails these athletes face every day.

MMA Worldwide Director Chris Staab poses with some of the beautiful faces of Tapout.

Cris "Cyborg" Santos having lunch at TapouT Clothing headquarters.

100   8839   100

Behind the scenes image of Bobby Pittman as he prepares to interview a Ms. MMA model prospect.

Bobby Pittman telling RJ Clifford you tell Dan Henderson of Team Quest that we're going to be late.

Bobby Pittman and Tapout photographer look through model pictures as Punkass watches on.

RJ Clifford finishing the technique pages.

As of October, 2009 Mike "Joker" Guymon became the 1st member of MMA Worldwide to become a UFC fighter.

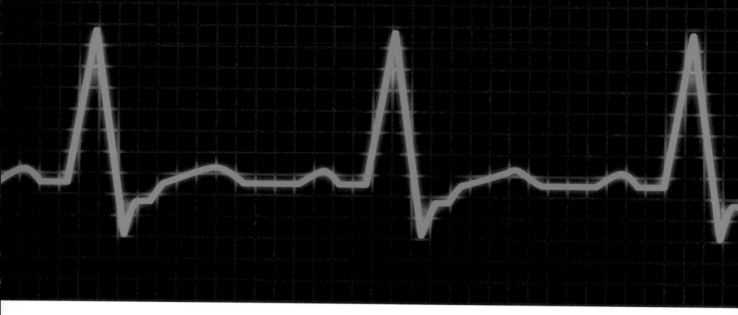

CHAPTER

MMA ANATOMY & TECHNIQUES

With both *MMA Worldwide* and *Tapout magazines* featuring the popular MMA Anatomy column and Technique pages respectively, it only made sense to include these segments in the TV show.

Each week pro fighters like Dan Henderson, "Razor" Rob McCullough and Rameau Thierry Sokoudjou give fans the inside tips.

Dr. Franklin Lowe, our sport's injury consultant, provides important weekly information about many common MMA injuries and how each can be treated. As the personal physician for the Pittman family and much of the staff at MMA Worldwide, Dr. Lowe goes above and beyond for all of his patients. He practices full spectrum Family Medicine with a special interest in Adolescent and Sport Medicine. He treats many athletic related injuries and has personally run 1,200 miles a year for the past 20 years. He always practices what he preaches and he firmly believes that exercise is the best medicine. Despite his hectic schedule he was able to add a very important segment to our TV show and we are forever grateful. **Dr. Franklin Lowe, from all of us here at MMA Worldwide, we thank and salute you.**

Both "Technique of the Week" and "MMA Anatomy" segments aired in all 10 episodes of the TV show.

Dr. Franklin Lowe, renowned sports injury physician, gives his weekly bit of wisdom to help keep athletes safe.

Cyrille "The Snake" Diabate
prepares to give viewers helpful
tips to improve their game.

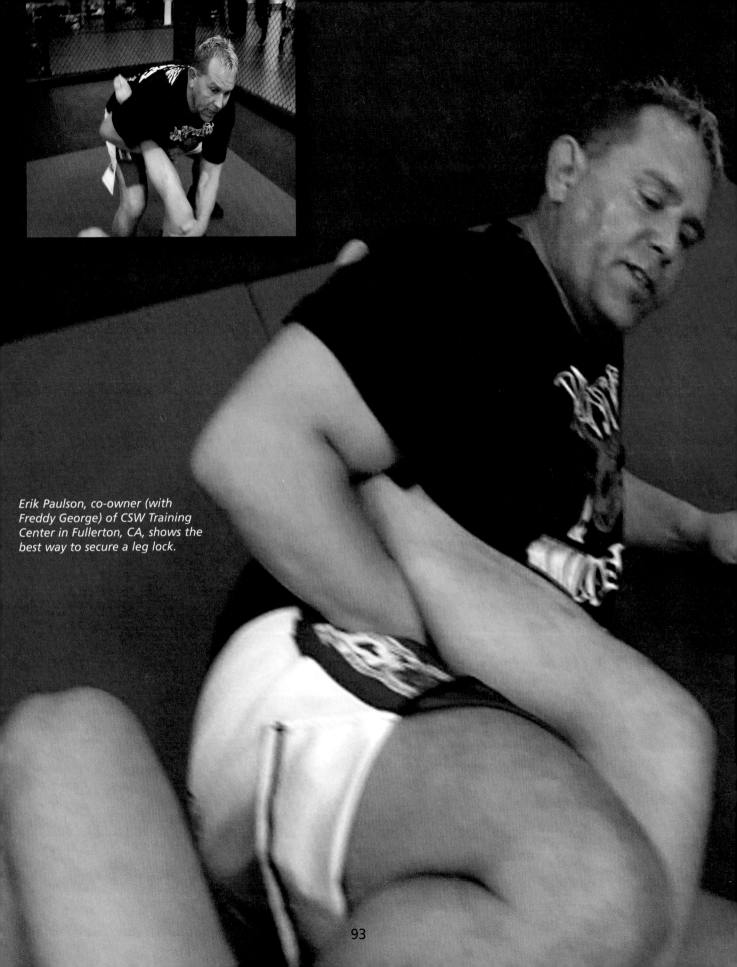

Erik Paulson, co-owner (with Freddy George) of CSW Training Center in Fullerton, CA, shows the best way to secure a leg lock.

"Razor" Rob McCullough prepares to inflict damage and shows

www.pridefc.com

PRIDE 男祭り2005
-ITADAKI-

YAMADA

フトワン

Moments after this photo was taken; Freddy's back hit the mat with a thunderous impact thanks to Sokoudjou's superior Judoka skills.

CHAPTER 14

OUTTAKES

Throughout the season, our cameras caught more footage than you could imagine. Even if an episode was three hours long, we STILL couldn't have shown you all the footage that hit the editing room floor. Some things just didn't fit the format of the show, while others made HDNET say, "There is no way we are letting this air!"

Thankfully through the Internet and this book, we are able to show you a few of the moments that never saw the light of day. First there was a moment like when Reggie Warren Jr. (a popular Internet MMA prankster) showed up to Freddy's gym. He was pretending to be Lyoto Machida's striking coach. When he walked into the gym (CSW Training Center), he was wearing pajamas and drinking beer. Freddy was not amused.

Also the crew learned a valuable lesson in Bas Rutten's backyard: don't steal Bas' Ionic Breeze! When the good folks at HDNET saw an amped Bas shoot two would-be thieves exiting his backdoor, they thought this might not be such a good idea to air.

"Razor" Rob McCullough prepares to blow fan's minds on take # 273 of Technique of the Week.

Freddy George quickly finds out that Bobby Pittman is no pushover.

Bas Rutten shows MMA Worldwide his new home security system.

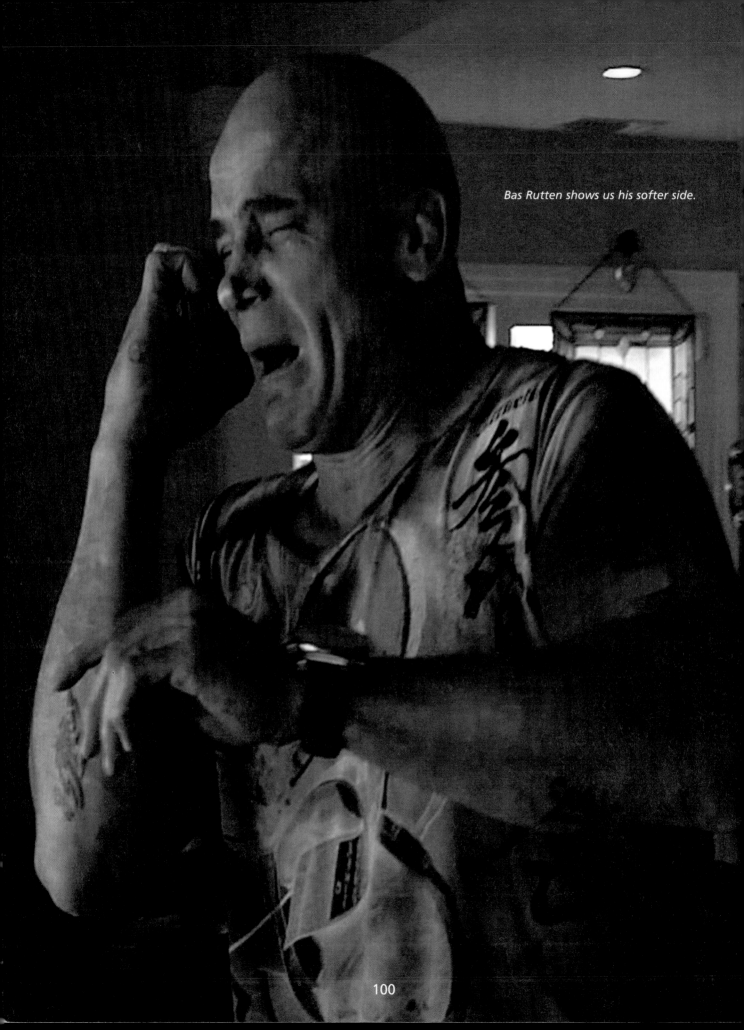

Bas Rutten shows us his softer side.

Frank Trigg shows one of our crew members a little tough love.

TUF *season 9 winner, James Wilkes,
plays his part in a spirited prank
against Freddy.*

Reggie Warren Jr., famous internet
MMA comedian, prepares to try
Freddy George's patience.
For this deleted scene
visit www.mmaworldwide.com.

103

CHAPTER

FUTURE LOOK

With a name like MMA Worldwide, you better have some reach…and we live up to our name! With nearly a decade of experience covering MMA in places like Russia, Australia, the Philippines and Hawaii, we are here to stay.

We are excited about the future of both magazines and Season Two of the *MMA Worldwide* TV show. We have a lot of irons in the fire these days and can't wait to continue the adventures of the MMA Worldwide crew!

In the upcoming season, we plan on travelling the globe to bring you stories about foreign fighters and trace the roots of some of the sport's most popular styles.

Mixed martial arts is not only the fastest growing sport imaginable, it's one of the most compelling sports in the world. As the heart of the sport continues to beat, MMA Worldwide keeps our fingers on the pulse. We will continue to bring you the stories that impact the sport in the most dynamic of ways and 2010 will be an amazing year. Stay tuned!

Australian fighters training on Bondi Beach.

Season 3 will take us abroad to countries such as Australia to cover the MMA scene

K-1 kickboxer Peter Graham and former UFC heavyweight Soa "The Hulk" Palelei square off in the cage.

Peter "The Chief" Graham cross-training for his transition into MMA.

Coach Chris Leben gives corner advice to one of his prized athletes Ricky Hoku.

UFC fighter Chris "The Crippler" Leben carries a heavy bag up to the top of Koko Head Crater in Hawaii.

Ms. MMA Worldwide

Diana Chaloux

Diana Chaloux is a WNSO Pro Fitness Model (World Natural Sports Organization), the reigning FAME Pro Fitness Model World Champion and Fame Pro Fitness Model North American Champion.

Diana is originally from the beautiful state of Vermont, but currently resides in San Antonio, TX. Fitness is her passion in life and she loves pursuing every angle of this industry. Her mission is to use her platform as a fitness role model in order to inspire, educate and motivate others to lead more fit and healthy lifestyles and to aid in the ongoing battle against obesity.

www.dianachaloux.com

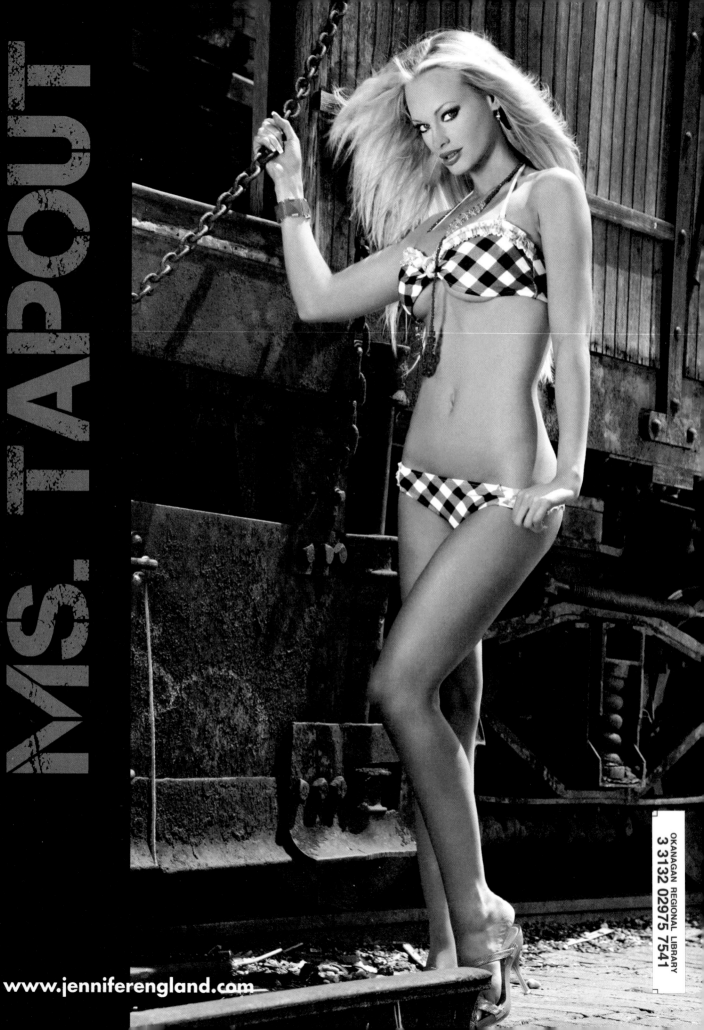

MS. TAPOUT

www.jenniferengland.com